We Adopted a Dusty Miller

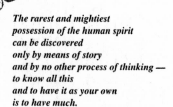

The rarest and mightiest
possession of the human spirit
can be discovered
only by means of story
and by no other process of thinking —
to know all this
and to have it as your own
is to have much.

GORDON KEITH CHALMERS

We Adopted a Dusty Miller

One Family's Journey With An Attachment Disorder Child

by Phyllis Bosley

Forward by Paula Vink-Cody, LSCSW

Illustrations by Tamara Bosley

Authors Choice Press

San Jose New York Lincoln Shanghai

Authors Choice Press
an imprint of iUniverse.com, Inc.

For information address:
iUniverse.com, Inc.
5220 S 16th, Ste. 200
Lincoln, NE 68512
www.iuniverse.com

Forward by Paula Vink-Cody, LSCSW
Illustrations by Tamara Bosley

Note: Some of the stories in this book have been changed to
protect the privacy and safety of the people involved.

ISBN: 0-595-13257-X

Printed in the United States of America

Introduction

---■---

This is the story of our family's adoption of a seven year old girl. It is my hope that the story of our adoption experiences will be of help to other parents going on this journey. I hope that the bumps and ruts, hills and valleys will be smoother because someone has read our story and will understand the effort it takes to parent a child who suffers from an emotional disorder. It was not until long after our child moved from our home that we learned about Reactive Attachment Disorder(RAD), Attention Deficit Disorder(ADD), and Fetal Alcohol Syndrome/Effect(FAS/E). Neither we nor the professionals we consulted knew how to identify these disorders nor how to help our child or family deal with them. We have observed that families who are trained to parent Severely Emotionally Disturbed (SED) children have a significantly less traumatic experience as they struggle to maintain balance in their marriage and family.

This is the story of our lives with our daughter who we loved and tried to help as she presented us with one crisis after another.

Phyllis

Acknowledgements

Although this is a story I felt I must tell, it could not have been published without the encouragement of many friends who listened while I got it together. My thanks goes to them, my husband; my daughter-in-law, Tammy, and Paula.

Foreword

As you read "We Adopted A Dusty Miller", you will experience first hand through the eyes of Phyllis Bosley the heartbreaking struggles of a family who had little knowledge of caring for a chronic maltreated child. Kristen, the Bosley's adoptive daughter, immediately began demonstrating behaviors characteristic of a child with severe pathology. It was a shocking reality for the Bosleys to discover that what would be considered normally practiced parenting skills were ineffective in dealing with Kristen.

The Bosley's expectations that their affections would be returned to them by their adoptive daughter were quickly shattered. This family's struggle is not unique to adoptive families, who are not prepared or trained in dealing with these traumatized children. The Bosley's attempt to find help for their daughter was unsuccessful. The knowledge and resources were unavailable, preventing effective treatment for Kristen. It was not until Kristen was out of the home, that she was properly diagnosed with Reactive Attachment Disorder and Fetal Alcohol Syndrome.

Recent scientific research confirms that nurturing and stimulation in the first 3 years of a child's life is crucial to brain development. This research has been instrumental in helping professionals understand the effects of early trauma on children. Our professionals are learning more about Reactive Attachment Disorder and how better to prepare adoptive families for caring for a maltreated child. This tragic inability of children to trust and love others is a severe disability, a disability of the heart.

The first step in preparing families for parenting a chronic maltreated child is to provide them with the child's complete history. Early childhood trauma can not be ignored. Children carry these permanently etched beginnings forever. Prenatal histories are important, from every substance the mother ingested during pregnancy, to the environment in which the child lived.

Our communities, teachers, clergy, medical professionals, therapists and social workers need training in treating and diagnosing Fetal Alcohol Syndrome and Reactive Attachment Disorder. We are becoming more aware of the need of adoptive families and their children. There are effective treatments available and excellent resources throughout the country, such as ATTACH (The Association for Treatment and Training in the Attachment of Children). However, these families continue to need increased adoption subsidies and post adoption services.

The Bosley family, despite their painful experiences, continue to support adoption. Phyllis has been a blessing not only to me but also to many adoptive families. She devotes her volunteer hours helping adoptive families find resources. She offers encouragement and support to adoptive mothers. Phyllis' desire is for families to have what she so desperately needed. It is through her story that she hopes to educate and give hope.

Paula Vink-Cody, LSCSW
Cedar Branch Family Services, Inc.

Dedication

━━━━━■━━━━━

To our sons in appreciation for your patience,
for never acting superior, for trying to help, for not
giving up on us, for going on with your lives through
the turbulence. Your successes gave us energy,
restored our strength, reassured us, gave us hope and
inspired us to endure. You are the medalists in this
complex undertaking.

Table of Contents

———■———

Chapter 1

———■———

The Dusty Miller Story

Let us imagine that a person has a dream that some day there will be a butterfly in their family. A butterfly which is perfect and beautiful. The butterfly will move gracefully from place to place leaving the scene just as it was when the butterfly arrived.

Now, imagine that instead of a butterfly a dusty miller arrives to stay. The characteristics of the miller are very different from the expected characteristics of a butterfly. The miller flaps and flops from place to place with no apparent destination in mind. It will land on anything that is quiet and it loves to hide in corners, cracks and crevices. When it moves, it may bang into anything leaving dusty marks in its wake. Usually it is attracted to bright flashy objects like light bulbs and pursues these dangerous objects to the death. It has no judgment concerning liquids and is often found nearly drowned in shallow pans of soapy liquid.

Attempts to re-direct the miller's frantic movements are ineffective. It does not seem to notice the family's endeavors to guide it to a safer place. Instead it considers any such attempt to be an attack and becomes even more agitated.

When a member of the family tries to get close to the miller, it becomes frantic, flying here and there. Should the person be able to get close enough to touch, the miller hurts itself in its panic and leaves a messy, dusty spot on the person who was clever enough to come close.

The miller leaves messes in out of the way places which must be cleaned by its family, sometimes with great difficulty. Due to the miller's practice of hiding, the clean-up period consumes an extensive amount of time.

Sometimes the miller arrives with many friends who have identical characteristics causing the family to go to great lengths to discourage them. Claims have been made that certain tricks and chemicals are effective for this purpose but no data has shown these claims to be true.

Close friends of the family sympathize but can offer no lasting help. People in distant places avoid coming near and suggest that the family has brought this invasion upon themselves. They are heard to say that a miller and its friends are no problem in "their" state. The family is forced to live with this problem with little relief.

Finally the miller is considered to be an unavoidable part of this family's life. No one gives attention to its presence until it is found again nearly lifeless near one of the cracks or crevices in which it formerly had hidden.

Now please continue this flight of imagination and consider the possibility that there is a little known method of changing the behavior of the miller in such a way that it will still be a dusty miller but will not continually leave messes nor will it pursue its typical self-destructive activity. This family is now in the position of deciding to what lengths it will go to make this possibility available to their miller. Life with this miller has taught them many things. They have learned to look with joy into the spirit where the beauty and grace of a butterfly has been hidden within the miller.

Imagine the joy of this family if and when that spirit is set free.

Chapter 2

———————■———————

It's Not So Much What We Did But Who We Were

Howard and I grew up in small farm communities in Nebraska, as did our parents and grandparents. Our parents' most pressing interest was children. All were involved with schools and youth activities. All were Protestant church members, and church attendance was important but reasonable. All our parents love to read and learn. There was very little conflict with extended family or neighbors. We knew our parents were respected in their communities for their generosity and trustworthiness.

Howard had one older brother and I had nine younger siblings.

We met when we were twelve and were assigned seats together in school.

Our first date was to a youth group meeting. His mother let him drive. She sat in the back seat. I was thirteen and he was fourteen.

We were married when he was twenty and I, nineteen. We rented a room, he enrolled at the university and we both went job hunting. My dad said, " I think they can live on love".

We made friends who already had children and went on picnics and outings with them and we enjoyed their children.

I was pregnant when he graduated. We moved to a small town and I was never employed again. I thought my job was to learn to keep house and build a family.

We were a unit within our extended families. Our parents were interested and supportive but respected our desire to "do it ourselves". Our marriage was forever.

Our family included three sons. A couple of months before our third son was born, I had broached the subject of adopting a girl. The subject came up occasionally during the next six years.

Our financial situation became comfortable and we felt we had the security, time, energy, love and space in our lives to add another child to our family. We also considered emergency foster care but wanted a more permanent relationship. We wanted to be in charge and felt that in foster care there would always be someone looking over our shoulders. When we applied for adoption we asked for a girl under ten, thinking that she would not take our youngest son's place. Our sons were excited.

As it turned out, the process took three years and she was younger than our sons but it occurred to us that she was conceived about the same time that we first discussed adoption.

Many things happened which we could not have dealt with had we not had the experiences of those years in a small town and years of interest in the works of Eric Berne and Muriel James and Dorothy Jongeward, especially <u>Born</u> to <u>Win</u>. During that time I remember praying for God to find a girl who needed us.

I believed then and more so now that God prepares parents for children, <u>not</u> children for parents. Our life experiences prepared us for some of the events that occurred later. For example I became comfortable around mental health professionals through a community group which organized a community mental health organization. This was the way I learned to trust enough to ask for help from therapists.

I wondered many times where God was during Kristen's first years, but I am confident now that God prepared us to take care of her during part of her life.

Paula has reminded me that the Hebrew translation of "adoption" is "planned in love for us." We are chosen to participate in God's plan for adoption.

Kristen

Kristen was born prematurely to Ann, a teenage mother, who was unwilling to identify the father. Ann was involved with alcohol as a teenager and for at least 12 years after. Kristen said other people called her a different name but she "was born being named Kristen." She and her mother traveled from husband to husband. There were two other children later whose fathers were accused of abuse and criminal activity.

For reasons I do not know, Kristen was sent to live with her grandmother for a short time. She was removed from her mother's custody at least once and placed in foster care. Her step-siblings were then placed with their relatives, but there was no suitable family for Kristen so she was placed back with Ann.

She told me about the police coming to her home. About being locked in a closet "when they had company." About standing in the street crying for someone to come change her pants. About being whipped with a belt when her brother cried. And about going to church with her grandmother. At home, I was told, her mother forced her to stand in a corner and pray to God to forgive her for causing her mother's problems. And she told me about the shocking sexual things her "father" made her do.

Kristen, at age 6, was placed for adoption when her mother had no one to turn to and was going into treatment. The grandmother was determined to be unable to care for her. Ann told her, "I don't want to see you again. Someone else will pick you up after school." The social worker picked up a frantic child who had waited all day for something to happen. The social worker had selected a few things from the house, but didn't take Kristen there. They went directly to the foster home therefore there was no opportunity to say "good-bye" or to gather any toys or clothing Kristen might have wanted.

All during the six months she was required to stay in foster care limbo, the case worker picked her up one day a week for an afternoon at a mental health center to deal with abandonment and neglect as well as to prepare her for adoption. We were told that in that time she conquered her fear of closed doors and the mental health worker was confident she would fully recover.

She always thought someplace else would be better. She was wildly excited to be going to a new family. The state rules assumed a get-acquainted period of several months which would give the adoptive family time to prepare and decide whether to continue the adoption plans. [Currently it is also assumed that therapy will be provided to help the child prepare for adoption.] Instead, the worker relented and placed her with us within three weeks of when we first saw her. This was considered adoption even though we had not gone through the court process, yet.

This child had been separated from her birth mother at least three times by age five. At least three men in her mother's life molested or abused her. Her actively alcoholic mother threatened for years to get rid of her—and did it. Beginning with foster care placement, there was no eye-to-eye contact between them for fifteen years. Twice in one year Kristen was moved to a different home, religion, school, and "family"! Both times Kristen's surname was changed. The relation-ships were cut off as if she became a new person with each move. After she was brought to us at age seven, she had no opportunity to say good-bye to her birth family and only two contacts with her foster family.

I learned about her history, the things she had endured, and in some instances, how she felt about them by listening to her play and her talk. She cried and talked for a couple of hours after she went to bed. In addition, she was always eager to tell people about her life.

I am so pleased that policies in the placement of children are changing to acknowledge the need for a transition time for children who must be moved from family to family.

First Impressions

As prospective parents our first sight of her was when she was peeking out from behind the case worker's skirt. She shortly made eye contact with her prospective dad and decided she would be safe with him. We met her in a large motel where there was a swimming pool. Twelve years later she was still thinking she had been cheated because she was led to believe we lived in a house with a pool. She could never get it straight even when we stayed in motels on trips.

She had a sort of nervous smile and eye movements which reminded us of someone we knew and was very charming. The case worker suggested that we take her to another town for our visit, where we would not be likely to run into anyone from her birth family. The caseworker feared they might discover where she was and what was happening to her. I think the suggestion that an adult who looked like Kristen might appear in front of me on a street stayed with me until I met the birth mother thirteen years later.

As we traveled down the highway, she was in the back seat (always in motion) and she talked continually. The chatter went something like this: "I don't know if I like them. Maybe today I will be able to find out what kind of people they are. I don't think I can like a Dad who has a beard. Maybe he will shave it off for me. If I tell him not to smoke maybe he will quit. She is fat but not as fat as she was. Do they have a big yard? I can't live in a house where there is no swing. I want to move today, I don't want to go back to the foster home. Can I call you Mom and Dad just for today? I just want to try to call you Mom and Dad to see if I like it." Etc. Etc. Etc. This chatter went on constantly for the entire afternoon. We took her to a park and tried to take a picture of her, but had difficulty catching her stopped long enough to get the camera focused. Finally we put her on top of the slippery-slide and one of us held her while the other took the picture.

Years later we were to learn that this incessant talking and familiarity with strangers were symptoms of attachment problems.

We had been waiting for three years for the call from the social worker telling us that there was a girl who needed us. At our first visit with the social worker, we said we would have to be assured that treatment was available where we live or it would not be fair to the child. The social worker made a call to the mental health center and arranged for us to take her in to see a specific person whenever we thought it was time.

We had some knowledge of adoptions that failed because the adoptive parents did not receive enough background information to enable them to respond to the child appropriately. So we asked to see her file before we saw her. This had been arranged and we had seen her picture. We knew that she had been emotionally abused and physically neglected. We knew she had been in therapy once a week for five months and had conquered her fear of closed doors, which, we were told, stemmed from being locked in a closet. The report was optimistic as to her being able to "settle down and recover in a stable home with siblings." Other information which was available in her file was not given to us until much later, too late.

The weekend after our first meeting, the case worker arranged for us to meet her along the highway at a rest stop and we took Kristen home with us for a visit. The case worker told us what she knew of the family background and the problems she saw that might come up. She'd spent one-half day a week with Kristen and had become fond of her. The case worker wanted us to know everything she was permitted to tell us.

That weekend visit was a picture of what was to come. Kristen was all over the place, never sitting still or even standing still. She was constantly talking, usually with her back to others and phrasing her sentences as if she were talking to herself. However, when she fell asleep, she slept quietly and for a long time. She played with our sons and did not seem to be shy in any way. She had several temper outbursts. One occurred when a poorly aimed rubber band was snapped and hit her arm. She screamed as if someone had shot her. Also, she got angry when she was told to wash her hands or to sit in a chair at the table to eat. Nonetheless, we were taken in by her charm and were ready to keep her in our family. We were so excited about her energy at the end of our long wait. We didn't know that her constant movement was never to pause.

Despite Kristen's pleading to stay, we took her back to the foster home where we were questioned and tested by the foster parents, Ed and Sally Jones. They told us they belonged to a church group which had broken away from another church and that Kristen had been saved and they didn't want us to mess up her salvation. Ed and Sally had asked their Christian friends whether it was okay for them to go along with Kristen being adopted by Presbyterians, and they decided that if Howard quit smoking we might be all right.

The Joneses told us things they knew about the birth family, and about the disciplinary methods in their foster home. Ed said they had to whip Kristen. [She said they used a belt.] They told us that this was the first foster child they'd had who didn't have to go back into the same situation she/he had come from. They told us Kristen had run a 102-104 degree temperature at least once a month and had a severe case of chicken pox while she was in their family. They told us she was very strong-willed; however, they had been able to get her to do her chores. They said that once she had been running backward and turned and ran into a picnic table and had to have many stitches taken in her chin. After we experienced her aversion to medical treatment, we wondered how they were able to keep her motionless long enough to put stitches in.

We came home expecting a couple of months for decision making. I sat with our sons and explained to them that if we adopted her, there would be a lot of shifting to be done. I compared it to making room in a church pew for one more person—every time we stood in church people would adjust a little and eventually there would be room for all of us. Our third son, who was only eight and one-half years old, had earlier made the comment that since we had six dining room chairs he would be happy they would all be full. I was so excited about having this little dark haired Kristen in our lives that I don't think I would have heard a warning if someone had suggested to me that there was trouble ahead.

Instead of the expected two months, we soon got a call from the case worker saying that Kristen was upset at having to stay in the foster home and was pleading to come to our home. The state had decided to rush the placement. We were asked to go to the foster home that weekend and pick her up. We made a makeshift bedroom and began to get ready. Again we recognized a sign of lack of attachment.

We took all our sons with us so that they could see where she had lived. We listened to the foster parent's judgment of our Christianity and suitability. We packed the few things she called her own and some the foster parents called hers. Her clothes were two sizes too small and her shoes were too small and falling apart. We learned that shoes never lasted long because of her constant movement.

The case worker was not available so someone who we had not previously met, gave us the permanent placement papers which we would need for medical care and school enrollment. In the signing of these papers her last name was officially changed to ours. We now had four children, sons ages fifteen, thirteen, and eight and an eight-year-old daughter.

Unfortunately, because Kristen was moved from one area to another, her file was moved and there was no state person who knew or felt any responsibility to us or her. We had only our own family and friends to support us.

Chapter 3

―――――■―――――

Family Adjustments

From the beginning of our life with Kristen, her impulsiveness and manipulation placed her in control of most of our life. It was a constant battle to maintain our roles as parents and her's as child. She often seemed to sabotage our plans intentionally and complained that I wouldn't let her take care of me.

It is difficult to describe the way Kristen acted. She was always in motion unless she was asleep. She moved her body as if she were jumping rope and hoola-hooping at the same time. She ran wherever she went. She talked all of the time. Demanding, complaining, giggling in a silly way. She cried as she was going to sleep, a mournful wail. Between moans Kristen talked loudly about what had happened that day or in the past as if she were telling herself what she was crying about. "I don't like it here, they don't have a hamster. I wanted to play outside, etc." Without her knowledge, I sat in the next room and studied what she was saying. I learned an awful lot about her that way which made it possible to cope with some of the behavior during the day.

Whenever anyone assumed authority for making decisions about what was going to be done, such as time to go to the store or what we were going to eat, Kristen became unreasonably rebellious. If she stubbed her toe or there was a loud noise she was angry because the chair tripped her or the door slammed "on me."

Another phrase she used repeatedly was "all suddenly". "All suddenly, I fell" or "All suddenly" someone was mad at her. She couldn't seem to understand what caused things to happen.

The first time she met people she was very likely to ask them if she could live with them. It was as if she were looking for the perfect mother who would never expect her to do anything she didn't want to do. Many times, she said, "I do what I want to do when I want to do it and I don't do what I don't want to do when I don't want to do it." Although this attitude was upsetting, I reminded myself that this probably was the way she survived her very early childhood experiences.

Her rebelliousness and our feelings of sympathy for what she had been through before she came to us were gradually wearing us down. Yet, there was never a time when she didn't seem to be better than she had been before. This fooled us into thinking that someday, she could function normally. Actually, there just wasn't enough time.

Meal time

Meal time was a trial from the first. The first day when she was told that she should sit at the table to eat, we were met with absolute defiance. The compromise was that she could take her shoe off and put her smallest toe on the chair while she ate. This continued for a couple of weeks. She ate enormous helpings of the foods she liked, such as mashed potatoes, macaroni, Jello and browned hamburger. Physically and emotionally she seemed to be bottomless.

She brought up crazy topics at the table, especially when others were having a serious discussion. Making statements which were ridiculously untrue or admitting to something she had done wrong. Or stating something she was going to do which was impossible to ignore. We learned that she could not handle people discussing a subject which she didn't understand, for example, the boys would ask Howard questions about calculus homework and she would interrupt in some manner. I thought she had probably been hurt by people who talked about subjects she didn't understand and the intensity, however slight, frightened her.

She panicked whenever something was spilled and I believe our lack of panic frightened her. Our response was "uh- oh, get something to wipe it up." She seemed to expect violence.

Eating out was a trial because of her constant activity, poor manners and conversations with strangers.

Cooking for herself was difficult because color-blindness prevented her from seeing when something was completely cooked.

One time at the dinner table she began to wail and sob because she wasn't born a blonde. Because we had been told that her birth mother thought Kristen's hair was ugly and also because we knew she had tried to imitate the foster sister's hair style, we hadn't tried to change her hair or get a good cut. But ultimately there came a time when she wanted her hair cut shorter. I told her I could trim it. She seemed very excited and we got the comb and scissors and pro-ceeded to wash her hair. Just as I began to cut, she ran out of the room yelling, "you will never do that to me, what do you think you are doing?" I calmly said, "Okay, I don't need to do this; we will wait until you are ready," and began to leave the room. At this time, she put her arms around my legs and dragged me back saying, "Don't ever give up on me, get back in here." We then proceeded with the haircut.

Sorting out Physical and Emotional Needs

For the first year or so she had a cold that would not quit. Her nose ran off her chin most of the time. Our doctor told me that she just needed to begin to feel secure. She had a high temperature once a month which was a little lower each time until it and the cold stopped. How I wish I had insisted on medicine to clear that up.

When, for a check up, she needed to have blood drawn she screamed, "You will never do that to me again," and her eyes rolled back like a frightened animal. It took four adults to hold her down. I wondered who had done what to her to make her react like that. This turned out to be typical of any medical procedure until we gave up on anything that was not absolutely necessary. By that time, I also had seen some angry, almost out-of-control doctors.

After several emergency room and lab visits we found that we could expect her to scream like this. We didn't encounter any medical personnel willing to use a restraint. More than a few of them stomped out of the room. One charged us extra because of the fit she threw about getting a stitch in a finger.

However, by trial and error, we found a dentist willing to adjust his routine so that she could receive necessary treatment; and finally a doctor who heard us.

When she was about ten years old, I left the children at home and went out for lunch. I received a call that Kristen was hurt and bleeding all over. I rushed home to find that she had slammed a door on her finger. The nail was loose at the cuticle but still attached. Our family doctor was out of town and I was able to get an appointment with a new doctor. He was willing to listen to me tell him how she was likely to act. He asked her to clean it herself and then calmly arranged her position so she could show him the finger. I held the other hand and he restrained her feet while he looked but did not touch the wound. She wrapped the finger herself and we left the office. It healed perfectly. It was the first time she had medical attention without a major tantrum.

We could perceive a bubbly, cute, energetic, interesting person peeking through all her anger, disappointment and fear. It seemed that being color-blind was just one more thing for her to cope with and it didn't seem fair. We began to think of her problems as a big onion; one of those sweet ones from my childhood. Each time one layer was peeled off and taken care of led us closer to the sweet center.

At the time of her arrival, I had lived with children all but three of my 38 years. I was pretty sure I knew what normal childhood behavior was and this roller coaster didn't fit my definition of normal. Given the limited history we had access to, we did not expect her to be able immediately to overcome her emotional problems; however, the case worker and the mental health worker assured us that when placed in a stable home with siblings, she would adjust. Unfortunately

the myth of a stable home healing emotionally injured children hangs on and prevents many children from receiving the help they really need.

After about two months, we decided that Kristen would need to continue therapy and she was taken to see the counselor. This therapy continued for about four years until the psychologist moved. He recognized her hypersensitivity and seductive way of relating to people. He listened to my endless stories and read my lengthy, wordy, written notes of what happened week by week. Unfortunately, the notes I gave him have nearly all been destroyed. He told me always to remember I was the Mom and to do whatever it took to maintain control. I felt supported by him. At one time, I asked him how many abused, abandoned, adopted children he had treated and he responded, "This is the first."

The first time I took her to see him, she climbed a tree in front of his office and I had to pull her down and drag her by her feet into his room. She hid in a fetal position in a corner under a table. The next time, she went in as if she owned the place and proceeded to try to control the sessions thereafter (she thought).

We received much instruction in time-out procedures, as well as going to the library to read up on behavior modification. If we could persuade Kristen to sit absolutely motionless, she would calm down eventually. But let a finger move and it all had to be started over. There was a time when she was ten when she was able to give herself a time out when it was suggested. She would look at her watch and stop moving for a few minutes. It seemed to give her mind time to catch up with her mouth and body. Within months she again would not consider stopping to calm down or think.

Our other children were each reacting in his own way. We tried not to give them responsibility for her and are thankful that we did not. They each were the object of comments about their strange sister. Some of their friends were especially supportive and one commented that what our family had done was "noble". (Maybe we wanted to feel noble. We had given a homeless child a home and family. We were struggling to find a key to help her recover from "overanxious reaction to early childhood" which is the diagnosis she was given.) We allowed our sons some special privileges in thankfulness for their tolerance and helpfulness. Many times we were cross and preoccupied when they needed our attention. When they did take her to places or watch her, we know it was not an easy task. She did whatever she could do to cause disruption.

A typical incident happened soon after she became part of our family. I had the idea that Kristen and I would have a mother-daughter evening and we would go to a high school girls basketball game. Kristen announced that "girls don't play basketball" but we went anyway. When we arrived at our seats she began to act as if she were afraid of me and said, "I am not going to call you 'Mom'." Then she left her seat and explored the area. Finally, I saw our elder son,16, across the gym and decided to ask him to take her home. She screamed at me while I took her hand and pulled her to the door. She refused to put her coat on so he tossed her over his shoulder and took her to the car. He tells us now that she used language so foul he couldn't believe what he was hearing. (We as parents did not hear any of this type of language from her until 10 years later when she was out of our home.) When she arrived home, she shut herself in her room. Howard didn't know what had happened so he tried to open the door. After a short struggle, she changed her mind, moved her foot and the door hit her right in the middle of the face giving her a black eye and a temporary crease in her forehead. After that, he was able to comfort and calm her for the night. The next

19

Sunday when we arrived at church, she told the first person who asked, "Dad hit me."

For 14 years we tried to parent her and tried to explain her bizarre behavior to schools, doctors, counselors, neighbors, family and friends. As we were trying to find help for her we found ourselves continually having to establish our credibility. I got increasingly more frustrated with the inability of people who I thought should know, to comprehend what I was talking about. I felt as if they immediately looked for something we had done wrong instead of trying to find the source of her problem within her. I haunted the library for some explanations which would indicate a solution. We tried various behavior modification styles, tried to "have more structure in our home." cried, got angry at her, and at professionals, and laughed at the ridiculous situations we got into.

"Are you 'just a parent'" was a phrase which signalled to us that we were not going to be taken seriously. I tried telling teachers what I knew. I tried asking teachers what they thought. I tried staying away from the school. Nothing made a difference. We felt convicted of causing this child's problems even though we had only been a very small part of her upbringing. We were asked, "Why do you keep her?" And some "well meaning" teachers went so far as to tell our sons that their parents weren't doing it right. Whatever it was!

It seemed that we were caught in a web of misunderstanding and were helpless to untangle it. As I came to realize that people would be only exposed to the bright cheerful side she showed to the public, I began to talk more and more about her and to hear more and more comments about what a nice child she was. This put me on the defensive until that is all I could talk about. Other parents find they don't talk at all about the child. Both reactions result in isolation and loss of friendship. I began to sit at the typewriter and pretend I was writing a letter to someone who would listen and help me make sense of all this. Getting it on paper relieved stress and helped me to resist telling everyone I met what was happening. Those pages formed the basis for this book.

Did You Really Mean To Say That?

These statements were made by people who considered themselves to be professionally trained experts. But, who, in all fairness, had little or no knowledge of Attachment Disorder, Attention Deficit/Hyperactive Disorder or Fetal Alcohol Syndrome/Effect. They were just trying to help. Sometimes we listened, sometimes we were insulted and sometimes we were left standing there speechless.

"If she can sleep all night, she isn't ADD."

"I think she is retarded because she doesn't mind moving to another place."

"I would say she is hyper-sensitive because activity in the classroom distracts her."

"Her actions are normal, my daughter was rebellious at the age also."

"Her grades (not test scores) show she doesn't have a learning disability."

"She isn't schizophrenic, she knows the difference between reality and fantasy."

"She seems to think there are two ways to act so she must be borderline dual personality."

"She is really smart; she listens to me with apparent interest."

"She is not very bright; she can't play card games."

"She is stubborn; I can't get her interest redirected."

"She is uncoordinated; she bumps into the wall in the hall."

"She should be playing sports; she is so strong and enthusiastic."

"She is very creative; she makes up strange answers to test questions."

"She is seductive."

"Her parents cause her problems; I don't have problems with her in my (unstructured) classroom."

"Why do you keep her?"

"Don't let her have a driver's license; she runs over curbs and doesn't like stop signs."

"Give her more praise."

"Are you just a parent?"

"She has ten strikes against her, she didn't deserve it, someone did this to her."

Amateur diagnosis was only confusing, never helpful.

Chapter 4

———■———

Survival

Howard and I were full of excitement for a long time, thinking that she was improving in her behavior, which she was. We put her to bed early and took turns leaving in the evening or reading jokes to one another to create that helpful laughter which is so necessary during times of stress. We tried to continue our interests such as reading, sewing, golf and working with Boy Scouts.

Juggling schedules around the activities to which we were accustomed was a monumental task. We took turns giving attention to each of the children. We didn't give up anything which was important to us but we gave less time and we had less energy for what we did. Attending meetings or running errands distracted Kristen from her need to control.

Our sons had no difficulty with school work and their social lives developed in different ways according to their varied personalities. All of them became Eagle Scouts during this time of turmoil. The elder two graduated from college and secured good jobs. One was married. One lived at home one year after Kristen left. One remembers trying to help Kristen understand that Mom and Dad were trying to help her. The other remembers learning that Dad had counted the knives and hidden the ice picks (how frightening that must have been). The youngest son, being less than nine months older, knows the details of living with an emotionally disturbed sibling. We asked him to take the responsibility of getting her to the school property in the morning. I told him he could stop the car and let her out anywhere, go on to school and call me if she became more than he could handle. To my knowledge he never let her out. We asked very little from him other than this important job.

The boys were successfully employed during high school years in a variety of part time jobs. One summer all four of the children were playing softball or baseball on different teams.

Through a church friend, we became aware of the book <u>Adopting the Older Child</u> by Claudia Jewett and were very comforted to know that many of the things our family was experiencing were typical. We loaned it to people who wanted to know about our experience. We asked our parents to read it.

Howard and I have a strong, long standing relationship. We seldom get angry and were able somehow never to become angry or discouraged at the same time. Dividing responsibilities and authority is typical of our marriage relationship and as parents, trusting that the other will do his/her best. I think we learned this from the example of our parents.

Searching For Support

Child Care

The constancy of trying to keep her safe when she was getting more and more angry, rebellious, depressed and sneaky was taking a toll on our emotions and energy.

In the evenings when Kristen was occupied with homework or play we would leave the house and just walk around our block. I felt short (and beat down emotionally) so I asked Howard to walk in the gutter while I walked on the curb. This was such a small thing for him to do for me but it was tremendously helpful in building my ego back up. We walked like this often even though we could only be gone a few minutes.

We hired a sitter for Kristen until she left our home at age seventeen. Actually, we arranged for her to be in a supervised environment with some therapy until she was twenty-two. Because she acted as if she were eight we felt it was not safe for her to be unsupervised.

We searched for years for a sitter who could provide safe supervision for her and not be conned into letting her do something unsafe. We found we could take her to the sitter's home and she would be distracted and not get into as many predicaments as she did at home. The time came, however, when Kristen discovered she could call and ask boys to come wherever she was and that ended the sitting stage.

When she was about twelve, we planned for a week to go to a concert. Kristen had a new dress and all six of us were going. We ate early and dressed to go. Two or three minutes before time to leave, she announced she wasn't going anywhere. She yelled and kicked and screamed. She said we would never be able to make her go to a stupid concert. We put her in the car and went late, but we went.

Another time we gave her the privilege of planning a family Saturday outing. Which she did very nicely. She planned a picnic and decided what time we would go to the park. But she threw a huge tantrum about getting in the car. We spent an hour persuading her to go and she pouted for 24 hours. [It wasn't worth it.]

I have spoken with many parents of children with an attachment disorder and most of them came to the resolution we did. We made family plans without consulting her, giving her no time to spoil them.

After a series of these incidents, we stopped telling her in advance that we were going out whether it was with or without her. We just explained at the time. She acted better and enjoyed herself more if things happened "all suddenly."

Professional help

We were by then seeing a counselor who never had any ideas about what we could do. She shook her head from side to side and listened to us and smiled.

For the first few years, we received no assistance from Social Rehabilitation Services (SRS) of any kind. Kristen was simply sent to our home. I called the case worker twice and SRS three other times. The first time, I asked the case worker to come to our home and meet the child she had placed with us. This was the case worker in our area to whom the file had been given. The case worker said she didn't have time but I insisted that she meet us for lunch "on us." She came and her only memorable comment was, "My, I don't know how you do it."

At the time, I felt Kristen had been neglected by the system and even abandoned. I knew how easy it would have been to be pulled into the abusive behavior which Kristen expected. When she was angry, she followed me around as close as she could get and accused me of abuse, plotting abuse, not loving her, not caring, being a bad parent and just wanting someone to hit. I understood exactly why someone had locked her in a closet, but I resisted because I knew that this was coming from her early experiences and most of the time I didn't take it personally.

I felt the lack of concern on the part of the state was dangerous to the child, yet at the same time I felt complimented that we had been trusted to take care of her. I certainly didn't feel like anyone was looking over our shoulders.

The second time I called the case worker was to ask her to delay the court proceedings until we thought the child could handle the trauma of going to court. Our lawyer handled the actual adoption when it occurred, and no case worker came to the court house. Years later, I spoke to SRS to receive additional psychological background. Another time, I asked for advice and assistance in handling Kristen's desire to contact her birth family again. This case worker cared and helped. We were finally given access to information about her earlier childhood which we had not known was available. The previous workers apparently thought it would be an invasion of the birth mother's privacy. It is our opinion that we should have been given all of the family history in the beginning so that we could have confirmed the stories Kristen told us.

Our other SRS contacts occurred when we sought help in getting out-of-home-placement and later having a guardian appointed. As I remember, there

were five different SRS workers over the years involved and all but one told us, when they did something, "I don't think my supervisor will approve." It
was as if any assistance or support the workers wanted
to give us would be against the rules. I believe atti-
tudes have changed greatly since then, yet have a long
way to go.

Our support came from a few friends, other adoptive couples and our wonderful family. Our parents
never doubted our word about what was happening.

Chapter 5

———————■———————

What Do You Mean,
Stay Out Of My Stuff?

*We are the kind of family that lays things around
until the next time we need them. We aren't in the habit
of keeping everything in its place. Actually, a lot of our
stuff doesn't have a place. But we are also in the habit
of thinking of things like shampoo, money, books,
clothes and litter as belonging to an individual. This
means that each person might have his or her own
shampoo in the shower, drink in the refrigerator, glass
on the counter, or maybe loose coins on the table. We
have tried to instill in our children that if it isn't yours
you don't move it.*

*Now comes into our family, a person who thinks
that if she sees it, it is hers to use, that she has a right
to anything in the house because it is "my house." who
does not put any value on her own possessions, who
cannot bring herself under any circumstances to ask
permission or to wait.*

*This set the scene for one battle after another over
"stuff." Each little battle in itself seems petty. For
instance, who thinks it makes sense to ground a child
for using Mom's shampoo? Who would understand
that all activity in a house would stop and turn into a
violent confrontation over a pen?*

*When we had guests, Kristen would often go into
the bathroom or the bedrooms and begin to rummage
through other people's things and use them or play
with them. If the guests stayed very long she would
bring those items out into the parent's sight and be
very obvious about what she was doing. She was*

sneaky about the things she used, took, or broke which belonged to brothers or Dad, but flaunted using Mom's makeup, jewelry or writing supplies.

She would take something whenever she left the house. This might be a pebble or a toy or her brother's radio. I learned to check her pockets, purse and backpack before she left the house. She became extremely good at hiding these things and taking them to school. As a result, the teacher would call and ask me to come with a couple of sacks and take it all back. I went to the school before school vacations and brought home the contents of her locker so that she would have gloves, toys, games, records, books, shoes, etc. at home when she needed them. I was always amazed at what I found. I insisted (as did the school) that she be present when I cleaned out her locker. She made a big scene in the hall about my getting into her stuff. I never figured out how she got her jam-box out of the house and into her locker.

I learned that pack ratting is common in adopted and moved children. I tried to make allowance for this little mind that needed to take some article with her. I knew that she had been moved from family to family and not been permitted to take her things. So some of this made sense; however, when it went on for years and became more like stealing, I tried to understand it from a different perspective. I now think that she had such a need to be in control that she couldn't compre-hend the rules society has made concerning other people's possessions. She wanted to be the one who decided what she could and could not do. Also, I believe that she really did not value anything she herself owned.

I expended a lot of energy trying to discover some reason or meaning in what she was doing. It seemed that there should be a big explanation for her attitude and I was sure that if we could find the reason, we could find a solution. Now it seems as with many other of her problems, where there was smoke, there was no fire. The smoke was just there.

She made up stories about where she got gifts according to who she was mad at or friends with at the moment. Our gifts to her were almost immediately broken, thrown out or she would "forget" who gave them to her and we heard her telling someone that she received them elsewhere.

The way she tells the truth as she wants it to be, concerns me now  that she is an adult. Her use of possessions concerns me now that she is a mother. Can she, so exclusively concerned with her own feelings and comfort at the moment, ever possibly learn to be a parent? I think not, at least not without help. I know she is motivated to do certain things to get her own way. And I know she thinks that what she takes or does does not count if no one sees her. I see no sign that this will change.

Looking back, I wonder what we could have changed in our lifestyle to have avoided some of those ridiculous battles over "stuff." I know that when we did make concessions and buy, for instance, a big family bottle of shampoo, that everyone was not happy with the brand and that she used it so freely that it was empty very quickly. There was no way to identify who was using up the shampoo unless everyone had his or her own. We finally had to develop a plan where if you didn't want her to use it, you had to take it to your room. Then if she used a whole bottle in a week, she

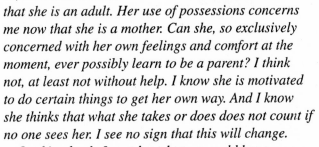

would be required to buy her own. But even these options did not work because as soon as one problem was solved, another came up.

We felt as if we were getting back to normalcy when she was out of our home and we were able to put our make-up and personal products in our bathroom and not have to lock them up.

I think there is a correlation between her attitude about things and her attitude about her body. Her sexual awareness took on a frightening aura when we began to suspect that she did not value herself enough to protect herself from exploitation or disease.

She could not perceive that men might have a commitment to someone who would be hurt by her aggressive seduction. People who observed her behavior with male strangers let us know that they did not want to be responsible for her in a social setting where someone's girl friend or wife might hurt (or even kill) her in a jealous outburst.

She had no respect for the rules related to dating. It meant nothing to her that a boy was someone's boy-friend. She called the guys her lovers and treated them as possessions, someone she could have when she wanted them and who would "save" her if she got into trouble.

Boyfriends were in the same category as "stuff."

Chapter 6

———■———

Why School?

School was Kristen's escape, her excuse, her albatross. It was too stimulating. It was too difficult. From kindergarten through high school there were constant problems. Looking back, we can find little to justify the work and aggravation involved in keeping her in school and trying to help her learn. At this time, we believe, top priority for an emotionally disturbed child is that he or she learns to get along with other people. Social development is absolutely necessary to any kind of success. It will not matter whether he or she can read if there is no ability to relate to people. This understanding puts homework in a lower priority than play or cleanliness, and lower than understanding of the feelings of the people we meet.

At the time when we were sending Kristen to school, we did not know how useless it was to try to get her to do homework or to keep up academically with other children her age. We believe now that she suffered from Fetal Alcohol Syndrome or Effect and came to a place academically where she had reached her potential.

We had been informed that she spent most of her kindergarten and first grade days in the nurse's office because she was so far out of control.

Second grade was the year she moved to our home. When I visited her classroom, she turned in her seat thirty times a minute and said, "Look at me, look at me." Her only success that year was memorizing a part for the class play. She also knew all the other parts but could not relate what the play was about.

She needed an audience to succeed. It was as if when no one was watching she could not function.

This was shown to be true when she had a job and would not work unless the supervisor was watching.

Third grade required too much self-control. The stress of trying to meet the expectations of the third grade was too much for her. She lost her concentration, coordination and cooperation. The therapist she was seeing at the time suggested that we enroll her in a new special class, Behavior Disorder, or send her to a hospital. She was the first student in the new class. There, with concentrated supervision, she learned a little. She worked on five problems:

1. staying in her seat,
2. staying on task,
3. following instructions,
4. minding her own business, and
5. finishing her work.

We will never know whether medication would have helped.

Fourth grade saw her transferred to a regular classroom with access to the Behavior Disorder teacher before and after school. The classroom teacher was firm and structured. Kristen did her work but she would not finish reading a story or a book. She always stopped a few pages from the end. The subject matter in the books was beyond her. She made few friends and was a very unhappy little girl. It was this year that we learned that she had no sense of direction. She could not find her way home from school.

During elementary school age we would go through weeks when she would do something just as she was leaving for school which would require a response from me, such as taking money to school or refusing to get properly dressed or refusing to eat, etc. etc. I would respond and there would be a screaming argument resulting in my holding her and telling her I would never give up on her. This was a forty-five minute ordeal after which she usually went to school and I tried to get centered again.

Other times, the tantrum would end in her taking a fetal position in a corner and wailing that her mother should have had an abortion. I think I might have done some good by holding her had I known to use the resolution time to bond. But the advice I received was to leave her alone to work it out.

I was not employed out of the home and although I had many community responsibilities, I was nearly always available when the school called for help. Howard was six blocks away and usually free to come and help. The boys most often had already left for school before the tantrums began.

In addition to the constant runny nose, there was the odor problem. She soiled herself and was indignant when she was asked to clean herself. She was required to bathe and launder her soiled clothing. She would not brush her teeth or use a deodorant unless I insisted and watched her. I know this must have been a big problem in the classroom and on the playground.

During Kristen's early school years, there were about four girls who would tolerate her long enough to make it through an hour and a half of play. This required of each of them a laid back personality and a mothering sort of attitude. Occasionally, one would come to me and ask me why she was doing what she was doing.

Play with boys was very unusual. It consisted of hiding under a tree or playing that the boy was a baby and needed her to save him (reminding me of the half-brother she lost contact with). As she got older, the boys she brought home were immature and played like she did, walking on the sofa and using bad language or necking in the back yard.

She was not able to play board games or card games because of her lack of knowledge and lack of humor. She was not coordinated enough to play ball or other outdoor sports, nor was she interested. Play involving music became so sexually suggestive that everyone was uncomfortable. The same lack of interest was true of crafts or hands on learning, cooking, sewing. She could not play alone because, again, she needed someone to be watching all the time.

Fifth grade required another change in schools. She decided the first week that the teacher didn't teach right. She wanted only one subject to be discussed at a time and demanded that the teacher not write more than one assignment on the board at a time. The teacher spent much extra time with us, but we never convinced Kristen to do any work at school. At school, she twisted her fingers as if she were trying to tie her hands together and when she got them just right, she couldn't pick up a pencil. She brought homework home and spent hours attempting to do it. I now think that she would have been better off playing and learning about how to get along with people.

I believe that it was the fifth grade year that she began to determine right and left handedness. We were still suggesting that she choose which hand she would eat with. Something was going on in her brain. Maybe the twisted fingers were an indication.

Sixth grade was one argument after another. There was a problem with noise in the hall which was distracting. She and/or her teacher called me often to come whenever they came to an impasse, however, no one would give me a bad report about behavior. In the spring we called a meeting at the school to discuss junior high. The teachers and principals concluded that Kristen was too "mature" to repeat sixth grade and assured me that there would be special arrangements made for her next year. The maturity they talked about was probably their sense that she was more sexually aware than other sixth graders.

Even though the school she chose was farther away, she chose it because she could walk straight down the street, therefore not getting lost.

In addition to her very capable verbal skills, Kristen used body language to express herself. For example, cringing, hiding, screaming as if in pain, flailing her arms and legs, and throwing her glasses across the room. At about age ten, she became more intentional in hitting out. I learned that I would get hurt if I tried to remove something she was holding.

One time she had gone to a girl's camp to help with the younger children and even after we had a discussion about not taking the other children's toys, she brought a fairly large toy home and hid it. When I discovered her playing with it, without thinking, I reached out to take it. She swung around with her back to me and kicked my shin so hard I thought I felt the bone bend. She showed no remorse. It took me a few minutes to recover. Eventually, she put the toy where I could find it and I returned it to the camp myself. The consequence was that she did not go back to camp and I spent a couple of days with an angry spite-filled child.

Her leisure time alone was spent getting things organized. She would rearrange her possessions or make meaningless charts of numbers or lists. Her Kleenex would end up in the jewelry box, old shopping bags in her notebooks, jewelry in her purses and money in her toy box, etc.

She was at least sixteen before she could sit and read a book with interest. This is about the time she discovered sexually explicit romance novels. We told her we would not allow them in our house. Girls brought them to school to share with her, she brought them home, I put them in the trash. One mother actually called me to demand that I stop doing this as the books were from her personal collection. My response was that as long as the trash came into my house I would put it where it belonged.

Television

Watching television was off limits for several years because she became so emotionally involved and usually took on the personality of the bad guy for sometimes days. Later, she would watch football because she enjoyed watching the guys. She wanted to be the one who decided what to watch and once she had watched for thirty minutes, there was certain to be a huge blow up over stopping and going on from watching television to some other activity even if it was something she had planned and wanted to do. She would change the channel to MTV whenever she had a chance and then go into a pout because her parents were preventing her from having a real life. She thought she was missing the party.

Kristen decided one summer afternoon that she should continue to watch television and eat a quart of chocolate ice cream. When she discovered I was not going to permit that, she ran down the street, picked up another twelve-year-old child and proceeded to the police department where she demanded to be allowed to file abuse charges. Howard had seen them going, followed them and was present. The policeman asked the little group to step into a room. He asked her what her parents had done. She said, "They won't let me have ice cream whenever I want it." He said, "Who is this man?" "My dad." "Do you love your parents?" "Yes." "Then go home and act like it."

We were beginning to get anxious about junior high. I spent hours calling residences and schools for girls. We searched for information about camps and treatment centers. There was no suitable place for her.

One summer, she went on a trip during which she proved that she could cope with some pretty complicated airline and bus travel, however the camp was socially disappointing and she arrived home dirty and smelly.

Later, she was asked to speak to a large group about her trip. She and I outlined what she wanted to say and she wrote it out in sentences. She practiced for a few days. On the stage, she watched the actions of the adults, copying them when it was her turn. She was able to tell the highlights of the trip and express her appreciation at a microphone in front of the large audience. This display gave me hope that she would be able to model after someone as she grew older. She was actually quite comfortable on stage and no one could have guessed the effort it took to get her there. Kristen always did outstandingly well in front of an audience.

During the elementary years in our attempt to achieve some form of discipline, we tried various forms of behavior modification. Her need to control simply sabotaged the effort from the first day. She would not try to understand the reasons for any of the items on the form. She was not interested in any way in the points or rewards. She tore up the form within 24 hours, hid it or refused to look at it. Even when we placed one of our boys on the same system and they participated fully, she would not consider it. Meanwhile, school and mental health professionals continued to suggest that we should use a point system.

We worked out a list of expectations which applied to all of our children. [The expectations of the therapists and foster parents trained by the Attachment Center are similar — everyone in the family is expected to work on being respectful, responsible and fun to be around.] Our list follows:

I made this list for her and explained that these are the things I expect of all my

~Messages~

1. Room neat   (Care of Posessions)
2. Dishes done on time (chores)
3. Respectful Speaking (manners)
4. Responsible Behavior
      (work, friends, Appointments)
5. Truthfulness
6. No Temper out Bursts
7. School work complete

© 1986 P.I

41

children. We discussed the fact that people will expect these things of all of us the rest of our lives. Six years later, a more comprehensive list was given to her as the condition of her living in our home. She refused to consider attempting to abide by these conditions.

Junior High Anguish

At the age of eleven most of the previously described behaviors were continuing. It was decided that a comprehensive evaluation would be done in the summer to gather the information we needed to enroll her in the Behavior Disorder program again when she began junior high. The doctors who evaluated her were very helpful verbally and explained the problems and needs very well to me individually. But these same doctors would not include in their reports the oral comments and suggestions they made to us. We could only get a brief outline of their records. The school administration therefore determined that she would not be considered for special help.

The principal was convinced that she would not have any problems "at school." At a meeting early in the year, he told the teachers to reassure the parents that Kristen had no problems "at school." The guidance counselor tried to build in some support for her, but we were aware the teachers did not feel free to tell us how it was really going.

Whenever I visited the school, I was treated with distrust. A former teacher told me this was because when a child has problems, usually the parent doesn't come to school and if they do, they are angry and they are really the cause of the problem. We were looking to experts for advice, yet, they couldn't help us help her.

Kristen's most successful class was taught by a teacher who was very organized in her personal behavior. The rules were the same every day, and the teacher's mood and expectations were consistent.

Fortunately, she was deemed eligible for a Title I reading class. The reading teacher took the time to test for the ways Kristen learned so the material was presented to her in a way in which she could learn. She made five years progress in three years which I learned was highly unusual at her age. A team approach to an educational plan for her probably would have produced good results, but that was not done.

Teachers for other classes refused to consider she had a problem and would not cooperate in a homework plan. They gave her breaks on her grades because she behaved well in class. We don't believe there was any academic learning happening outside the reading classroom. In fact, when I asked her what science was about she could not think of anything. When I asked her what she learned in science, she said, "If you don't sit still you have to sit under the teacher's desk."

Socially, junior high years were almost a disaster. Kristen thought a man in a blue car was going to save her from her life. We were asked by the school psychologist to take her and pick her up from school rather that letting her walk.

She met a girl who had beaten her mother with a chair and had been sent to a detention center. The girl told Kristen the center had a swimming pool and from then on it was a goal to get sent there also. She said the other students told her that she not only had a right, but a responsibility to hurt her parents.

Kristen was cheerful in the school building and completely angry as soon as she stepped out of the building. She became convinced that her family was keeping her in a jail and keeping her from her real life. On one occasion, she called another student and asked him and his friends to bring their weapons and take care of her parents. They didn't come, but we spent a few uneasy nights. The discussions precipitating these kinds of outbursts were usually about homework, breaking the rules related to other people's property, or personal hygiene.

When confronted with the difference in her school and home behavior, she said. "I have to work so hard to behave at school that I have no energy left to behave at home. I have to blow up somewhere."

From age seven to twenty, school and residence personnel were still saying she had no problem "at school" or "in our facility;" however, evidenced by their calling us and asking us to help, we knew better. During junior high, the school psychologist met regularly with her on his own time and attempted to help her cope with school.

Kristen attended one community dance for her age group. When she arrived home she was crying, continuing on most of the night because she thought her true love was there and just couldn't find her. She never forgave us for bringing her home that night.

I felt that it was up to me to help her find some peer activity. I made sure that she attended Sunday school, Girl Scouts and any sports she could possibly succeed at. She loved being part of a team and was the best one to encourage the others to play harder. Sometimes she would have good coordination and could hit a ball, especially in volleyball. Because she was so strong, she could serve pretty well, sometimes too hard. She almost never remembered to go to practice or to a game, and any little thing would distract her during play. We went to her games and cheered her on. It was difficult to sit and listen to students calling her nasty names from the stands. But Kristen thought they were the only ones who were having any fun. She did not have any interest in spending even a small amount of time with well-behaved kids and she said the smart ones were boring.

Control Battles/How Do You Cope?

You've managed to get through a week of angry remarks, resentful comments. foul language and similar types of behavior. You've controlled your own resentment and used a calm, quiet manner as you explained that you could not fulfill every demand from this child.

You have cooked healthy meals for the family. You have avoided complaining to your husband just in case he might over or under react. You've picked up the house and almost completed the laundry, all the while attempting to focus your thoughts about which discipline method might be successful with this one child.

Discipline and praise methods with which you parented your other happy and confident children only seem to cause more anger in this child. Even the counselor's suggestions have appeared to make things worse.

About this time, the angry one arouses from the stupor of television watching and announces "you better get yourself in gear and help with my homework or you are going to be sorry."

Of course, this is the first time you heard about the homework and it is 15 minutes before your friend is picking you up to go out for a soda. When she arrives, the child is slamming doors and accusing you of not caring.

You leave anyway but have a hard time following the conversation because you are wondering how you will pay for repairs to the doors and hoping your husband will come home and handle the situation so you can take a shower and go to bed without the usual bedtime turmoil.

High School Brings Social Craziness

The next step was high school. The guidance counselor was so sure that we would "lose her" when she transferred to high school that she worked around the system to get her back into the shelter of the Behavior Disorder classroom.

Again, there was resistance from the teachers to cooperating with a daily report. Kristen surely did not really learn anything in those years, but had good enough grades to get a regular diploma because she behaved in the classroom.

By this time, we had three reports from IQ tests: age eight, 42; age seventeen, 71 and age twelve, 92. This is an average of 68.3 which seems close to correct and is also typical of fetal alcohol damage.

A few years earlier, a doctor who tested her had suggested she was the "opposite of a dumb blonde." She could express 80% of what she knew and understand 10 to 20% of what she heard. She was very charming and people seldom knew she didn't know what they were talking about.

She spent her time between classes running through the school, carrying notes from and to the special education students keeping them matched up with "lovers." Finally, the special education teacher and the BD teacher worked out a plan where she would not pass in the hall when other students did. Otherwise, she did not have time to get her books and get to class.

Kristen had no interest in changing her behavior, nor did she see any need to study. Her diploma is simply a memento of the efforts of many people who helped keep her in school. It does not indicate she learned any academic material.

At the time the diploma seemed important. We thought, like most parents, that graduating from high school was a high priority. As it turned out, no amount of education could make up for the inability to have or understand the relationships between people. I know she had no idea what it meant that her parents loved and cared for each other. If anything, she interpreted friendship and closeness between people as strange and boring. The people she called friends were people she either could manipulate or who would not object when she hung around them. Almost all of the people she called friends in her teen years have spent some time in jail or are living with someone who has been in jail.

I could see that the friends Kristen invited were trying to relate to her, but that she did not know how to play. Her play consisted of running from thing to thing or thought to thought. She tried to lead all activity and would get silly and loud, wearing out visitors quickly. Then when she saw that they were going to leave, she would focus her anger at me and ignore them, calling me names and being rude and offensive. If I tried to intervene and direct the play to some activity that was more age appropriate, she would become very angry and rebellious and again fling insults at me. This was more than most visiting children/boyfriends could handle.

When it came time for school dances, she could not think of anything else. She ran all over the school trying to get a date and to match up everyone else. At the dance, she was so silly and wild acting that no one initiated conversation with her. She ran around talking to everyone and having a good time. After, at home, she was angry and hostile as if she thought the dance was still going on and we were forcing her to miss it.

It was apparent that the prom was going to be a problem. She was panicked about getting a date. I was told that she wrote notes to every boy in school saying she would do anything if he would take her to the prom. She did very little school work and was absent from the classroom occasionally because she was so busy trying to get a date for herself and anyone else she thought needed help. Finally, a teacher called and suggested we should keep her home because she had made so much trouble some boys' girl friends would hurt, if not kill her, if she showed up at the prom. Fortunately, there was an alternate prom party to which she was invited. She had a really good time; however, she and her date did not remain in the room. She did not seem to understand the program and activities which were planned.

These weeks were deeply sad for me. I knew that this was another indication that she would probably never be able to participate in "normal" young adult activities. I wanted to be able to take her shopping for a prom dress and to help her plan for a wonderful time. I felt cheated for myself and for her. That awful sadness and feeling of being cheated lies under my anger at the society we have developed which encourages one kind of personality and has no patience for those children who don't have the mental, physical or financial resources to participate.

A Different Place to Live

At the end of her junior year her daily angry outbursts, insults and threats to hurt us with a weapon and her depression were forcing us to look everywhere for a place for her to live and finish her schooling. Her acquaintances and her defiance were not only frustrating, they were frightening.

In the middle of one temper episode she called the local girls home and warned them that she was going to be sent there. "My mom is going to call the police tò have them pick me up and bring me down there so get ready for me." I had no idea that I had that option but upon learning that they had recently received their emergency foster care license, we quickly made the arrangements, without involving the police. She stayed there for a year at our expense. The fact that she was not in state custody, but was a private-pay client made us the case managers which turned out to be an awkward arrangement. Usually, the parents would not have had a say in most of the decisions. Also, the group home staff would have called a case manager, not the parent, when there were problems. The staff had the same problems with her that we had experienced, but with a little less anger and of course they worked in shifts.

The staff at the girl's home used a point system which, of course in her case, did not mean a thing. They were, however, able to get her to school and keep her supervised most of the time. When we visited, she was verbally abusive to us. When we didn't visit she called and insisted we bring her something or take her somewhere. "It is snowing so bring your sled." We didn't. Every one was assuming that with structure and love she would be okay. Having her out of our home, but near enough to supervise gave us the breathing time we needed to think things over and get a new perspective.

When she was 18, we admitted her to a hospital for further evaluation and medication. A week into that hospital stay she went out the window with another patient in the night. The hospital called to inform us that the police were looking for her. I sat in our dark living room waiting for them to call back. I thought she would be hit by a truck on the highway and I would need to be able to plan a funeral. I planned that funeral before they called to say they had found her in a truck stop. I believe that dark night was therapeutic for me in that from this time on I was more calm about what might happen to her. I believed she would run again and be killed in an accident. It was not until I faced the real threat of AIDS that I stopped thinking in terms of a highway accident.

After she was safely out of our home and in a residential facility Howard confessed to me that he had been sleeping lightly for a year with the fear that she would get up in the night and we would "wake up dead." The next step would have been to lock our bedroom door. This is when I learned that he had counted our knives periodically and hid the ice picks. Actually, he was correct. The "weapon" she had threatened to use to take care of us was a large craft knife which I kept in my art supplies and which he didn't know I had. We found it in the things she packed to run away with.

Howard had come to the end of wanting to parent her about a year before she left our home. He was waiting for me to come to the same point. That year of waiting was traumatic for him.

I am very thankful that she didn't have the creativity to think of any other way to hurt us. She truly believed we had kept her from her life. She watched MTV in other people's homes and thought the partying she saw was the way she should have been allowed to live. This conception was the reason she wanted to "take care of us."

During one year, she almost succeeded in never letting us see her smile. I actually went into the school building intentionally to watch her laughing and enjoying herself. She stopped when she saw me and became angry and abusive. But the smile I had seen gave me encouragement to keep on when she was threatening and demanding.

I was called to the school early one morning. I was not informed of the agenda. The problem was she had told a different story about her plans for the future to each of several people. She was going to get married. She was going to Utah to join the Army and receive $2,000.00. She was being sent to an institution. She was enrolled at a business college. She had a job. She was going on welfare and moving in with Jody who had informed her that if she touched Jody's boyfriend, Jody would kill her. All of these stories were untrue;

however, the adults who were interested in her life, were arguing about who was correct. Finally, they were all accusing us, her parents, of not helping her with her plans. No one had asked us. People were just assuming she was functioning as a high school senior who could make plans. In any event, I recognized Kristen's knack for setting people against each other while she went on her merry way. Some people left the meeting still thinking she had told them the truth.

One day, I found myself driving down the street imagining a picture of myself carrying a five-inch thick, 24-inch in diameter round jigsaw puzzle made of solid oak and with no frame. The puzzle represented Kristen's life. I had my arms around the outside of it holding it together out in front of my body. I knew I could not relax my arms and I could not transfer it to someone else. My arms were tired, my back hurt; yet I had to go on holding on for an indefinite time. Another low point.

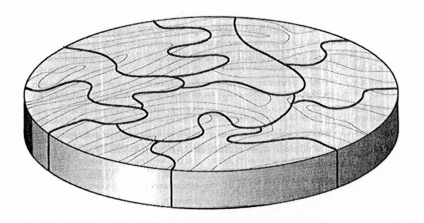

In spite of our hopeful intervention, reality or reason set in that this child was not ever going to be able to accomplish her dreams. Even the simplest events that others take for granted were going to be unavailable to her. Kristen seemed to come to that conclusion along with the rest of us, but instead of facing reality, she began to get better at deciding how things were going to be and behaving as if they were that way. This made it more difficult for me because I do not like to pretend. I wanted to be able to lower expectations and go on at the more realistic level.

Lowering Expectations

Gradually over several years, we began to stop trying to guide her toward some higher standard. We shed tears for her lost future. Tears of disappointment for her. Tears of frustration when other people thought we should be doing one thing or the other for her. Tears of fear that she would hurt one of us or herself in her headlong charge into what she thought was freedom. Tears of disappointment in friends who could not understand. I kept going on, doing the things I thought would actually make a difference. And I began to see myself as one big blob of sad. I was so sad for her, but could not dream of expressing that sadness to her. Howard was gradually pulling away from her and any emotional involvement with her and to a certain extent with anyone else. In blocking her out, he was also numbing his feelings and sense of humor. Ten years later he can still say his enjoyment of simple moments are dulled. At the time of her high school graduation we were at the end of the road as we knew it. We couldn't help her anymore.

We were now looking at the probability that she would never be able to work or live on her own. We began to research the possibilities of supported employment or Supplemental Security Income (SSI).

This was a low time for all of us. We could not see how this was going to end.

For years, I had carried a canvas bag containing Kristen's important papers and documents so I would have what I needed. One day, I took it to the SRS office, said I had to talk to someone, and placed it on a social worker's desk. I told her I could not carry it alone anymore and she would have to help. I remember laying my head on her desk and crying when she acted sympathetic. She took the time to listen, to get to know Kristen and to go out on a limb to apply for General Assistance for her. I was having no luck finding a place which would consider Kristen's application for group home residence. The response I got was "Are you just a parent?." This social worker made the calls which resulted in an application being accepted. She also met with Kristen in a conference setting, and she tried to bring out some cooperation in planning for the future. Everyone cooperated but Kristen.

About this time, Howard and I decided that we could not both work on the same parts of this puzzle. He took on the application for SSI and I the residence problem. That spring, one of our sons became en-gaged, one graduated from college and one from high school and I had my 48th birthday.

Division of parenting responsibilities was essential. The trust we had in one another again carried us through.

In A Corner/The Cycle

A note to the court appointed guardian

Sometimes when she is confronted with something she doesn't want to face or gets caught breaking rules, she has what we have called a tantrum. This is a period of days or weeks which follow a pattern similar to that described by Claudia Jewett in <u>Adopting the Older Child</u>. The angry or resentful mood lasts for most of this time. As this stage is winding down, she decides that some man is hers. She tells people she is going to live with his mother and his mother will take care of her until he "gets out" or "gets well." The mother has probably never met her. Usually, the man knows nothing of this plan. She puts all her effort and thought into this fantasy and uses it to try to get out of taking any responsibility for whatever it is she doesn't want to discuss or face. Finally, something happens and she has to admit the plan is not real. When this happens, she goes through the final stages of this tantrum by being quiet and acting depressed and follows that with a period of good behavior. These cycles began about age thirteen and continue to the present. I counted 8-12 repeats of this pattern in one four-year period of time.

Sometimes this "good" period is followed by a lot of talk about taking control, going back to school, getting a job, or finding new friends. Almost always she will begin telling everyone she is good in math (untrue) and is going to take algebra so she can go to college. She reads about three pages of the algebra book. She states, "This book is stupid, who needs to know about sets anyway." Thus ends the good period and the cycle begins again.

Chapter 7

———■———

Adult Living Arrangements

When it came time to leave the girl's home because she was 18 and had finished high school, a comprehensive hospital evaluation was again accomplished. The recommendation was that Kristen not return to our home. The SRS social worker assisted with the application and she was placed in a coed residence associated with a mental hospital. She was not only the youngest resident, but also one who was functioning socially and emotionally as a sexualized ten-year-old. She managed to keep the staff and clients in turmoil. Someone burned her clothes and for the first time in 35 years they had to call the fire department for a deliberately set fire. Two times, men tried to kill her because she was flirting with three men and calling them all "lovers." It was later discovered that during the fifteen-minute staff meeting each day she had been in bed with one of the "lovers." The staff at this residence had never been asked to deal with anyone like her. They saw the strikes against her and had no way to deal with her. There was a one sentence allusion to Fetal Alcohol Syndrome (FAS), but no follow through or explanation of what that might mean. We had no idea what that diagnosis could entail.

A kind psychiatrist informed me that parents are not required to take their adult child home. When we considered the threat of violence we were facing we decided to refuse to take her home. She stayed there two years because no one could find an appropriate alternative placement. By this time she was 20 and was receiving SSI because of her inability to keep a job.

Her job history was that she interviewed well, accepting the training with enthusiasm. Then when the training was finished and she was asked to work independently she refused to work saying, "Hey, this is my job, if you want me to do it your way, don't leave and go do something else." She would not work with no one watching her. As a consequence, she was fired time after time.

The experience of supported employment was the same. One day on the way home from work she lost or gave away or spent (she didn't remember) a $500.00 paycheck. Current research tells us over 80% of adults with fetal alcohol syndrome cannot handle their own money. Kristen would ask for a loan, spend the money and then refuse to pay it back because it was gone.

When she was a young teen, she would stare at the want ads and insist she was buying a car, never seeming to realize there was more to it than staring at the ad. She ran away from a residential facility and stood in a used car lot saying she was buying a car. She had no money, but she thought that standing there would be enough.

In the meantime, I was traveling 150 miles weekly or every other week to meet with staff for twenty minutes after they met with her. I would anticipate greeting her with a hug and she would usually ignore my presence. Howard took off work to go along when there was a planning session. At these sessions, we, Kristen, and the staff listed her strengths, needs, and possible plans to accomplish change. The group picked one or two things which Kristen thought she might try to accomplish and the meeting was complete. This was a waste of time accomplishing nothing except aggravating my stomach problems. As many other parents do, I began having physical symptoms when Kristen was out of our home. I believe they were a result of sudden relief of daily stress.

When I remember those sessions, I long for the chance to go back and do a wraparound case plan with input from more people. I would build in a way to monitor compliance on the part of all involved. I think this would have given us some indication or hope that something was possibly going to change. As it was, I didn't feel we had any power, that Kristen was just playing the game with no intention of working on her life, and the staff had no reason to be motivated to provide any more than supervision.

Whenever we called her, she interpreted our call as interference just because she wasn't the one who decided when we called. The staff complained we were saying something to upset her. Again, she managed to set the people who were trying to help her, against each other. Children with attachment disorder are masters at splitting and dividing staff and family.

It was at this time that we took the trip to reunite her with her birth family.

Chapter 8

———■———

The Adoption Nightmare

Let's be honest about it. Lurking behind and under all the joy and excitement, work and pleasure of adoption is the nightmare that another family will appear and claim a part of your child. When adoption occurs with an older child who has been in the care of the birth mother then that nightmare is increased significantly. From the day we first saw our daughter, her birth family and their friends were a part of our consciousness.

The first visit took place with the possibility and fear that the birth mother might see us. We were told she "looked just like her mother." Kristen made it clear she was comparing us to not only the birth family but also the foster family. She said, "You are really bad, but not as bad as they were."

She talked from that day on about her little brother. Whenever she spoke of him her arms went out as if to embrace him. When she met strangers, she told them first about her little brother whose care had been delegated to her. We knew someday she would have to put her arms around him and know he was grown and safe.

She became upset many times when something reminded her of them and incidents from her past. There was so much anger when she talked of her birth mother that we came to believe she could never heal emotionally until she had the opportunity to look her in the eye and ask whatever questions came to her mind. I told her whenever she asked that some day I would make sure they met again. Eventually, I asked what she would do if her birth mother came to the door. She said, "I would say, 'Come in here woman, I have some questions for you'." I then told her that I would have to know what those questions were before I could begin to do a search. The questions she came up with were so normally typical for an adoptee that I felt we must let her have some contact. I was nearly certain I could do the search myself from information Kristen herself had given me.

We received a letter from the state saying the birth mother had contacted them saying she would be open to some contact. This was a big shock. Up until that time, I had been able to think that the other mother had died in an alcoholic stupor and now, I had to face the nightmare of her living existence.

After consulting some people who specialized in adoption we decided to exchange letters through the state with addresses deleted. The letters were disappointing and few and far between. Kristen worked on her letters for days. We finally worked out a plan whereby she could tell me what she wanted to say as she read the letter she received and I would take notes. Then she took the notes and wrote from them. This was very difficult for me because I wanted to express my anger and to find out if the brother was all right.

Eventually, there was a letter from the half-brother and I wrote to him. I dreaded to get the mail because of the emotional toll each bit of correspondence took.

When Kristen was old enough to have the legal right to her mother's address, we went to a post-adoption worker and explained the situation. She, too, was overwhelmed with the possible problems which might arise. It was at this time we obtained the remainder of information from the file. We decided it was up to the birth mother to give Kristen information about the sister she knew nothing about. I came to believe that some of the feeling of being lost originated in the fact that these girls were close in age, but were separated as preschoolers. Later, her mother did tell her about the third child whose custody she had also lost.

Kristen often had nightmares. For example, she would dream she was in the water between two ships and the people on the ships were fighting so no one could save her. Or she was between two Indian camps and they were shooting arrows over her head fighting over who she belonged to. I asked her one time, "Who won?" Her answer, "You did. That was where the love was." Moments such as those are treasured in the midst of turmoil.

Dear Ann:

Hello! I think you will be surprised to hear from me after all this time. I was once your daughter nine years ago for most of seven years. We had fun in those times. We went to the park and played many times.

There also were bad times I would never forget. Times when people got hurt or our pet died. That hurt me a lot.

I know you are probably sorry but I can't forget how you hurt me. The fact is that the way you treated me really hurt. Now I know that you could not take care of me. I don't know why but I guess you had to give me up.

I have some questions I want to ask you.

Who's my real father? Do you have any baby pictures of me? Was I premature? What did you do when I was born? Where did we live? Where is my brother now? Why did you give me up? Are there any medical problem in the family I should know about? Where did I start school? How long did we live places? Why did we move?

I'm doing great now. I like school. I have a good family. I have friends who seem like sisters to me. I can't think of anything else to say. If there's any questions you want to ask me be free to ask.

> *Your long ago daughter*
> *Kristen*

Finally, a letter arrived which contained a phone number and Kristen and Ann talked. There were conversations with the brother and grandmother and mother's boyfriend also. By this time, Kristen was not living in our home. Kristen was determined to get her hands on her brother and use her first mother as a refuge from accepting responsibility for her own actions. She insisted they would take her into their home and everything would be wonderful.

I had always said that I hoped Kristen would be in an institutional setting when she met her brother again. As it turned out, this actually happened. Her half-brother had run away from home and somehow discovered she was in a hospital. He hitchhiked to the hospital and refused to be turned away until he talked to her. They spent one half day together talking, she said, about their memories and their mother. I considered this a gift from God. I think he was taken into custody that evening and there was no more contact for a few years.

After Ann had made and broken several promises to come to visit, we decided we would take Kristen to visit her. It was an eight-hundred-mile drive one way. Kristen was very excited, of course, and we were in a daze. I felt as if I were in a space somewhere between the Twilight Zone and Disney World. This could not be happening, and I wanted no part of it; but I had no choice but to do the right thing and get through it.

In preparation for our trip, I had arranged a meeting through the church and considered hiring a private detective to check out the situation before we got into it. I had no idea how any of us would react to this reunion and I was not sure I could get through the day. I was scared and thought I would be too angry to handle a conversation.

It was Kristen's 20th birthday. The family expected us to come to their home and stay overnight! It was absolutely out of the question! We met them at a church and did not tell them where we were staying. This

minister at the church was a very small woman who had
with her a dalmatian larger than she was. She had called
another minister who was a police chaplain and would
be wearing a badge. She was a little afraid also. They
arranged for us to use several rooms in the church.

Right on time, they arrived, mother, grandmother
and boyfriend. Seeing Ann was a shock to me even
though I knew that there would be physical similarities
and had heard the voice on the phone which sounded
just like Kristen. They recognized each other and
mother and daughter hugged while Grandma was
complaining that she wanted a hug, too. I felt good
about this part of the visit because I thought Kristen
acted more mature than the other two. I could see that
Grandma was going to be in the middle of things so
she and I talked for a while. Her explanations and
excuses were disgusting to me.

I suggested that Kristen and her first mother go into a
smaller room. When I saw that Grandma was going also I
stood in the doorway for a time watching and preventing
Grandma from interfering. I watched my daughter and
this other woman walk down the hall ahead of me like a
couple of identical twins. Incredibly, they had their hair
fixed the same way and that as well as their identical
body language and voices was so unexpected that I felt as
if I had left my body. I stood there leaning against the
woodwork near the door and knew I would run if I could;
but I couldn't. At that moment I was only a shell and
there was no breath or strength in me. I thought I might
fall and I did not want to fall in the room with them so I
slowly moved around and out the door into the hall where
Grandma was still talking a mile a minute about how she
just didn't know what went wrong with her daughter.

As we came into the coffee room where the others
were standing Grandma was continuing her talk about
the shrine to Kristen she had in her living room.
Finally, one of the ministers told her she should realize
that I was going through a stage of grief and she would

have to find someone else to talk to about her feelings about the adoption. She immediately went into a tirade about how she didn't have any problems and she wasn't going to talk to, "No one."

During this time Howard, without my knowing it, had gone out and taken a description of their car. Later, we learned that the second minister had done the same.

When we all gathered again at the door and they had our permission to take Kristen for the day to their town and home, I was unable to think of anything to say.

Howard put his arm around Kristen and said, "I have a canned speech. Kristen and I have talked about this and we have agreed that everything that is said today will be the truth. And if you aren't here with my daughter by 9:00 tonight there will be a three state alarm out for you." The look on the boyfriend's face assured me that they would bring her back to us.

They left in their car and we said good-by to the minister and went back to the motel and slept for several hours. We then took a tour of the town and ate a terrible meal. We found ourselves back at the motel with nothing to say but with minds full of questions. Finally, even though it was early, we got in the car and headed for the church again. As we pulled on to the highway from the motel, we realized that we were actually following their car. We could see Grandma and Kristen bouncing around talking in the back seat. It was such a relief to know that they were going to be back when we were.

When Kristen left their car to come to us, she stood with her back pressed up against Howard as if she was home. Again, I was totally speechless. The last words were from her first mother, who leaned toward me and said, "Thank you, you did a good job."

On the way home we listened to the activities of the day. At one point Kristen said, "I don't think they told me the truth because I remember it differently." It seemed that she forgot that thought soon after and began to see them as a wonderful escape again.

Chapter 9

———■———

A Chance For Freedom

During this time, we requested a guardian be appointed for her. The guardian was highly qualified but not highly experienced with this kind of personality. Guardianship took the problem of our having "her money" out of the picture. Actually, getting this appointment was not difficult to do with her history of hospitalization and group homes. It was extremely helpful and a great idea.

Eventually with the help of the guardian, she moved to a less structured residence. The original plan was to be a twenty four- hour supervised home, but Kristen convinced everyone but her parents (who by now had no vote) that she should be given a chance for freedom. So she went to a semi-independent living arrangement. She had an extremely difficult roommate who tattled on her every move. Despite this situation, she managed to "entertain" young men at three different times of day. She and each of them thought they were going to get married. In spite of her absent sense of direction, she learned the city bus system very quickly so that she could rendezvous with these men. She met a woman on the bus who felt sorry for her and invited Kristen to her family Thanksgiving dinner. There was a resourcefulness coupled with charm which she used to get what she wanted.

When she was confronted one too many times by the staff about her absences, she ran to the apartment of one of the men she was seeing. As it turned out, he had heard that his guardian was coming the next day to have him returned to the state hospital. Present in the apartment was another young couple with a baby, who thought someone was going to kill them. Kristen walked into their plan to take a U-Haul truck and leave the state. Which they did.

We were informed about her leaving with a boy-friend. During the next days, we calmly went on with our lives assuming that we were correct in thinking no one would want to live with her for more than two weeks.

The little group traveled around for a few days and ended up in a homeless camp where the young couple took off with the truck and Kristen and her friend slept in a pickup topper, with no pickup, until it toppled over. At this point, Kristen went for help at a place called Crazy Joe's. The owners made a big point of being Christian and informed the guardian they would take good care of them. The next morning; however, Kristen and friend were deposited at a shelter for the homeless.

The friend by this time was having seizures due to lack of medicine, so the shelter insisted that she take him to a hospital. While sitting in the waiting area she remembered my telling her she could only call collect if she was in a hospital or jail and she called us. She had been missing for fifteen days.

There followed a few crazy days during which she and her lover had a fight over a blanket and he tried to kill her and he threw away her birth control pills. Also, she was admitted to the hospital for an infection and gave his name making it difficult for us to find her. Someone had told her that if you live together for a week you are common-law married.

I made some calls in an effort to have her returned or to reassure myself she was safe. When the police took him into custody to protect her, we made arrangements for her to fly back to her guardian. This involved a very expensive one-way, short-notice airline ticket. During the four hours it took to make those arrangements, she already had found another man and wanted to bring him along. "He is so sweet. He was in the Gulf War and flew black widow planes." "If he can't come with me can I bring his things?" I told her the airline wouldn't allow her to carry someone else's luggage.

We made a rushed two-hour trip to meet the plane to see that she got to the guardian. She came off the plane in dirty clothes she had found in the Salvation Army discards. She had a paper bag in each hand. One had a teddy bear on top and the other a roll of toilet tissue. The first thing Howard said to her was, "What is the deal with the tissue?" Her response was, "Hey, where I've been, you take your own.." She smelled terrible and we felt sorry for the person who had to sit beside her on the plane.

The ten-day stay in the guardian's home was an eye opener. The guardian said Kristen drove her crazy. When asked what Kristen did, the guardian said "absolutely nothing." She was determined never to do what people wanted her to do.

The guardian placed her in an extremely small house hardly more than a studio apartment. —Alone. Kristen immediately began to refuse to do anything healthy or responsible. No sleeping at night, no cooking, no job hunting, and definitely no birth control.

Meanwhile, through an unusual set of circumstances, someone suggested I go talk to their friend Karrie about Karrie's child. When I did that, she sent me to talk to Paula, who had just returned from a training on therapy for Attachment Disorder. Paula gave me Foster Cline's green book, Understanding And Treating the Severely Disturbed Child. We read it in the car on the way to see the new housing arrangements. By the time we arrived, we were absolutely convinced Kristen's problem was Attachment Disorder. It was like reading a story of our lives. We had an answer to the question about why she was so angry at me, why the need for control and freedom.

We took her out to eat, bought her an electric skillet, bought her cat food because it was starving, and we looked over the house which had no food.

In our conversation, I tried to explain to her that eventually everyone has to do something even if it is only to put food in his or her mouth. She said she would never again do anything she didn't want to do. She said it was very, very hard to figure out what people wanted her to do so she could be sure she wouldn't do it. And she said she would kill me if she didn't think she would go to jail. At this point we ended the visit and returned to talk to the guardian. We reported that Kristen had not gone job hunting and the birth control appointment had not been kept. We purchased and delivered condoms. We left with the understanding that we would never initiate contact with her again.

It was a few days after this visit that we met with and informed the guardian and SRS workers that Kristen was so threatened by our contact that we would only answer her letters and talk to her if she called.

The next time we heard from her, she informed us she was pregnant. She had tried to convince some guy's mother to take care of her. This woman threatened to call the police if she came on her property again. So Kristen set out in the night and before morning had found a man who she had not previously known who would share an apartment with her and act as if he was the baby's father. This was as close to her dream of a husband and home as she ever came. Her fantasy was that when you became pregnant you automatically had a husband and a cute house.

Miraculously, this man took good care of her, and she followed his instructions to take care of herself and the baby. He is the only person we know of who could tell her what to do and get away with it. He helped purchase baby things, insisted she get exercise, good food, and sleep at night. He insisted he would leave her if she entertained men while he was gone. When the baby was born, he was at the hospital. He got up at night to take care of the baby.

During this time, she bought a $200 car which ran a week, long enough that she could drive it to the Driver's Examiners Office three times in one day and finally convince them she should have a license.

During junior high she had taken driver's education two times and the second time received a license even though she had refused to stop at stop signs or open the manual. She assumed rules were made to specifically spite her. We took the license and told her we would give it back when she could pass the written test. I told her I would never ride in a car she was driving and Howard told her she would never drive a car he owned. As a result, she didn't get back the original license.

One day when the baby was a few months old, she decided to try to contact her birth mother again. She called the Salvation Army and they put her in contact with her birth mother. She packed a suitcase, took the baby and went by bus to visit Ann and former boyfriend who was now her husband. Kristen had no interest in the furniture or the man she left behind.

Another miracle occurred when she arrived. Her birth mother and her husband took her and the baby in and cared for them for almost three years before Kristen again demanded her freedom and abandoned them and her baby to go on the street where she said she again "had her freedom."

Although we have come to terms with the fact that her problems are probably beyond anyone's ability to understand or correct, we still wish she could be safe. And we care that the baby will be safe and well taken care of by the birth mother who now has custody.

Chapter 10

————————■————————

A Glimpse Of The Future

Kristen was so closely supervised that early sexual experimenting was delayed, but it was clearly evident from the age of ten that her sexuality would be a problem. We have since learned that it is typical of girls with fetal alcohol damage and/or early sexual abuse to encounter this problem.

I could see that her impulsiveness and careless attitude toward the feelings of others would make it difficult, if not impossible, for her to parent a child.

When she did have a child at age 22, She could not maintain the mother role other than to brag about what she was doing. She left the man who was helping her with her child with not even a goodbye and was clueless when people asked her what he thought.

She spent 2 or 3 years living with her birth mother and her husband before the situation became difficult and they helped her find a place for her and her son to live. She developed a serious infection and, during surgery to repair damage, she was sterilized with her consent.

When it was discovered that she was entertaining many men and was not providing her son with food and drink, he was returned to Kristen's mother's custody. Kristen then began writing bad checks, continued having parties, and was evicted from public housing.

She began living on the street at age twenty-eight, eating at the same shelter regularly and moving from "friend to friend."

She has falsely reported abuse in an attempt to see her son. I imagine the situation with her son has brought back her anguish over losing her little brother.

A case manager has been assigned who has helped restore the SSI; but Kristen is not interested in permanent housing. Taking care of a household would require her to do the things that people want her to do.

She has found responsible adults who will respond when she wants to talk, much as she did with us as long as we didn't expect any reciprocity on her part.

We have asked to be able to help someone find suitable living arrangements for her where she will be safe and can work to support herself. We have always felt that she could work to support herself if she were in a twenty-four-hour supervised setting. She is obsessed with freedom; yet, cannot make safe decisions for herself when she has it.

The limits of confidentiality people work under will probably prevent us from contributing any information or assistance in finding such a place. Our involvement would require her requesting it and we know she is not likely to do that.

The extent of drug and alcohol involvement is unknown to us, therefore we cannot predict the next stage in her life.

Chapter 11

———————■———————

Explanations

Attachment and fetal alcohol damage

The writings about Attachment Disorder were so
descriptive of what we had seen in our daughter that we
were reaching out everywhere for more information.
The more we read and the more people we talked to, the
more we came to believe that this was the problem. As
we learned about the therapy that was being done and
the reasons for it, we could see the connection to what
we had wanted to do. Specifically, I had never been
happy about the decision to send Kristen immediately to
school. I had wanted to keep her at home and hold her
until she felt like mine. I did rock her, and when she was
angry I held her until she became calm. But I was told
to send her to her room when she calmed down. How I
wish someone had known to explain to me that that was
the time to cement the bond which never really developed. I didn't know it wasn't just me who needed to feel
as if she were mine. Now I know that to heal she needed
to feel I was hers. She needed to know that I wouldn't
let her hurt herself by going it alone.

My instincts surely came from my mother. She held
her children when they cried, when they were hurt.
She held them when they were angry. I don't ever
remember her saying "go to your room." She said over
and over, "It is okay, it is going to be better." I can't
believe I let people tell me to send this child to school
immediately. At school, she could avoid the reality of
her life and our love for her.

Not having a transition time into our family was a
major mistake. Not having a transition time from one

family to another was a mistake. In 1977, did anyone know?

At the time we were discovering the attachment literature, I had the good fortune through a miraculous set of circumstances to meet another mother of a child like mine. A support group had been formed which I began to attend. Eventually, I began to take the responsibility for gathering this group. My conversations with more than 70 sets of parents has confirmed my belief that an entirely different style of parenting is necessary for these kids.

As I listened to these women at least one a month for several years, I heard them tell my story. I found them living my life and speaking my words. On occasion when a mom came to the group whose child had a different emotional disorder, she was sure to realize quickly that she wasn't dealing with attachment issues.

The parents of children with attachment disorder problems nearly always tell the same story. They don't have any problems with their other children. Dad usually doesn't see there is a problem nor do grandparents and aunts and uncles. Mom is screaming for help. They have already been to several places for help. The child may have been diagnosed as Oppositional Disorder, but that doesn't really fit. Many are afraid to sleep at night. Many have locks on the doors in their home for the safety of the other children and themselves. Their child has stolen from them. Many moms have had to call the police to report violence or vandalism. There are concerns about sexual acting out and fires set in the parent's bedroom. Yet few people will believe the mother when she says this charming child is terrorizing the family. Marriages are in trouble or already broken.

I refer to the support group as a miracle as month after month when we arrive, the right moms come and are able to support the mom who needs help the most.

When I first began facilitating the support group, I tried to plan a topic or agenda, but it was no use. I believe it was God's answer to prayer which brought the right people to help one another.

Grief and stress take a toll on these families. Their signs are difficult to recognize and to face without help, yet families sometimes are too overwhelmed with the constant crises to reach out.

As marriages continue to falter and our children who did not have the advantage of therapy grow up to spend time in jail, are homeless, unable to keep a job or handle their own money, we are working to support the type of therapy and preparation for adoption and foster care which we believe will allow other children to grow to become "respectful, responsible, fun to be around adults".

We came to understand that the source of much of our distress was that our society does not believe it is possible for a child to have a severe emotional disorder. For this reason society looks to the parent as the cause. Even we ourselves do not want to believe the problem is in the child and we keep hammering away trying to find a solution or blaming ourselves.

My Definition of Attachment Disorder

It is important to keep in mind the process by which a child fails to bond. My definition of attachment disorder is as follows: The human child from conception knows instinctively that a mom is supposed to take care of the child's needs. When something happens, the absence of the mother for a period of time or some illness which is not diagnosed and dealt with such as ear pain, the cycle necessary to build trust is broken. The child believes adults cannot be trusted to bring relief when he or she calls out in rage for food, diaper change, or any of the other situations a helpless child might be in. A child who cannot trust must control all situations. And, I believe, that child will not be able to play. This child doesn't have much of a sense of humor or very little conscience, and because of an inability to understand cause and effect, cannot accept blame or praise leaving traditional styles of parenting useless.

As the child grows, the frustration and stress of having to control everything and the impossibility of the task causes intense anger to boil over into many relationships. The harder the person who is filling the role of mom tries to get close and bond, the more afraid the child becomes. And if the child begins to bond and release some of the control to an adult, the child becomes desperately afraid to lose the most important aspect of his or her life-control.

The skilled therapist who can lead the child to let go of control and rage so that the child can be a child and permit mom to be mom is hard to find and when found is in great demand. The families spread the word of success when they find this kind of help.

Our children are very good manipulators. They can spot a "bleeding heart" (someone who will take their side against the parent) in a crowded room or across the street. There is little that can be done to undo the damage done by a "bleeding heart." The temptation for the parent is to isolate the child from others and, therefore, isolate the family.

Violence comes and goes with little pattern or predictability. Foster parents, as well, find that these violent events keep everyone, including the child, on edge and "waiting for the other shoe to drop." A complete evaluation and an accurate diagnosis is required in order to fit the therapy and parenting style to the situation. There are a number of organic causes which may add to the violence. Seizures complicate the disorder and are sometimes not readily identifiable. Therapy for these children requires a united front at home and outside the home. Therapeutic foster homes are usually required while the child and parent learn a new way of relating to one another.

I strongly encourage parents to establish a paper trail, to keep a journal of everything and include copies of any reports or evaluations or test which are done. Parents should find out the history of the birth parents, and question until they are confident the social worker is revealing all the information. If the child may have trouble finding employment, don't delay application for SSI and other training which may be available.

Finances

Another problem which most families face is financial. The cost for this child with or without treatment can range upward to a million dollars. Adequate insurance coverage is rare. Travel cost to treatment is rarely covered. Medication, hospitalization, evaluation, tutoring, child care, legal fees, counseling for parents and siblings, damage to houses and absence from work add to the cost. Because most adoptive families are not informed of adoption subsides and biological parents aren't eligible, many families have thought they had to relinquish custody of their children to get the treatment which is necessary. Still relinquishment does not guarantee the child will receive proper treatment. Usually, when the child is removed from the home, the family is left to fend for themselves in dealing with grief, loss, guilt and the physical and emotional effects of sudden relief of stress.

In addition, we cannot ignore the cost to society of a child who has no conscience. Not only is treatment available for these children; the federal government is encouraging adoption, and funds are available for adoption subsidy. It will be the responsibility of the parent to secure this help for their child and their family.

The value of a nurturing support group for parents is immeasurable. Exchange of understanding, information, and moral support is of great assistance. Knowing you are not the only family facing these problems is an aid to reintegration and recovery of the family.

Treatment which actually is appropriate for a child can cut the costs in all areas. Accurate diagnosis and understanding treatment for the entire family can make a huge difference. When a team approach is taken and friends and community take part, the cost is reduced even more. Left alone, parents are nearly submerged in constant daily traumatic problems.

Fetal Alcohol Syndrome/Effect

While watching television one evening we stumbled on to the 20/20 program about Fetal Alcohol Syndrome/Effect (FAS/E). The experience was stunning. We recognized many of the signs Michael Dorris and Ann Streissguss spoke about. We were reduced to tears. It was the first time we had any knowledge of FAS/E. I immediately purchased the book, The Broken Cord. by Michael Dorris. The unusual thought process, the lack of cause-and-effect thinking, the math disability and the vulnerability in relation to strangers fit. Later reading from Ann Streissguss's work and listening to stories from other parents confirmed the fact that problems handling money and socialization are very common.

Now, several years after she left our home and supervision, we are able to fit all of Kristen's problems into a pattern which is understandable when abuse is also taken into consideration. It is probably too late to make a difference in her life; however, it is not too late to provide help for the other families which include a severely emotionally disturbed (SED) child.

I have come to believe that this combination of attachment issue's and fetal alcohol damage is one of the toughest childhood problems this society will face in the future. We must come to understand them and to work wherever we can to prevent them. They are preventable. To ignore them is a tragedy.

Chapter 12

———————— ■ ————————

Facing The Challenge

Can you do it? Sure!!

If you are thinking about adoption of a special needs child, you are wondering if you can do what it takes. Let me say that all the time you are parenting these children you will be thinking that you can learn just what you need to know to do it perfectly. You will lower expectations in some areas and open up whole new areas in your life and theirs. The danger is you will focus so much on how to do your part that you lose yourself.

It isn't "let go and let God" but "let God take responsibility for God's part." You will learn to trust that God has not given you a job you cannot do.

The wonderful things you learn in this time of your life will be with you and be a treasure which will enrich your life. You will pull that treasure out of your box to help yourself and many others as you live the rest of your life.

Chapter 13

———■———

Relinquish?!!?

An essay in honor of some of the parents I have met.

Relinquishment? What do you mean, relinquishment? Do you know what that means, have you thought this through? Why don't you go home and think about this for awhile? We can make an appointment later and we will help you think this through. Are you sure you know what you are doing? Is this too quick a decision?

After years of being the responsible person for this child, we have decided we have had enough. We have studied all the possible options. We have been told that what we think <u>must</u> happen to keep this child safe and from bringing harm to another person, is just not possible under the law. Doctors have given up. Social workers have given up or have refused to listen and take any responsibility. Insurance companies have refused to finance any more treatment, at least treatment which is helpful. Group home staff is worn out. Schools are unable to cope.

Despite all that, people still expect us to continue to fill in the gaps, make up for the cracks in the system, and take the blame for whatever happens. We are told that we are the experts and the counselors for this child and therefore it is up to us to find help.

Genuine love for this child, deep caring for this child, and an overactive sense of responsibility have been combined for many years to keep us going farther and farther into the unknown of the legal system and the psychology field.

We have come to the conclusion that there is no more that we can do as parents and that the best thing that can happen is for this child to know that no one is going to try to change her. It is time for this child to know that we have made a decision that will stand and not be changed, we think that the time has come to take this stand. We talk to our family and friends, and we consult with professionals and other parents. And we take the stand to love this child forever, while we step back and let her take control of her life and be forced to take responsibility for her decisions.

Suddenly, it seems to others, we have decided to let go. Suddenly everyone scrambles to get us back on track. Surely, they think, these people won't leave us in charge! Surely, they are just having an emotional crisis. Surely, they don't mean what they say.

Suddenly, lawyers and police officers and judges become involved, and people who have been helping the parents are now forced to take a stand. Blame and accusations are tossed around. People have to admit that they don't know what to do either. Eventually, it boils down to the bare essentials; this child will have to live within the law or pay the consequences.

After the confusion which our decision has caused settles down, we find ourselves relaxing, doing the little things that we have put off until she was better. We feel so good that we feel guilty about it. We dismantle his/her room, we take down the pictures; we place this child back into the corners of our hearts. Sooner or later we find that our child has fallen down and been able to pick up and go on. Our dreams and expectations take on a new look. We begin to hope that someday this child will be able to acknowledge the love we have for him/her and be able to respond by caring for someone other than self.

Until that time, we wait, hold our stand, and continue to love.

Suggested Reading

Berne, Eric, *Transactional Analysis in Psychotherapy*

Bowlby, John, *Attachment And Loss, Volumes 1-111*.
New York: Basic Books, 1969, 1973, 1980.
Pioneering work describing children's behaviors and feelings — the implication of loss of maternal bond on children.

Bowlby, John, *The Making and Breaking of Affectional Bonds*, Tavistock Publications, London, 1979.

Burchard, J.D., S.M. Burchard, R. Sewell, & J. VanDenBerg. (1993). *One kid at a time: evaluative case studies and description of the Alaska Youth Initiative Demonstration Project*. Washington DC: Georgetown University Child Development Center, CASSP Technical Assistance Center. (202) 687-8803

Cline, Foster W., M.D., *Hope For High Risk & Rage Filled Children*, 1992.

Cline, Foster W., M.D. & Jim Fay, *Understanding & Treating The Severely Disturbed Child*, 1979.

Delaney, Richard, Ph.D. *Fostering Changes: Treating Attachment Disordered Foster Children*, Walter J. Corbett Publishing, 1991.

Dorris, Michael, *The Broken Cord*, Harper And Row, Publishers, New York, NY, 1989.

Fahlberg, Vera, M.D., *Attachment and Separation*, Spaulding for Children, P.O. Box 337, Chelsea, MI 48118.

Fahlberg, Vera, M.D., *Journey Through Placement*, Perspective Press, P.O. Box 90318, Indianapolis, IN 46290-0318, 1990.

Hage, Deborah, *Therapeutic Parenting. It's A Matter Of Attitude*.

James, Muriel & Dorothy Jongeward, *Born To Win*.

Jewett, Claudia L., *Adopting The Older Child*.

Jewett, Claudia L., *Helping Children Cope With Separation And Loss*, The Harvard Common Press, Harvard, Mass., 1982.

Journal of Child and Family Studies, entire issue on the wraparound process, edited by Rusty Clark, Ph.D., and Richard Clarke, Ph.D. March 1996. (212) 620-8468

Keck, Gregory C., Ph.D. & Regina M. Kupecky, LSW, *Adopting The Hurt Child: Hope for Families With Special Needs Kids*, Pinon Press, 1995.

Magid, Ken, M.D. & Carole McKelvey, *High Risk: Children Without A Conscience*. Bantam Books, 1988.

Magnusen, Debbe, *It's Never Dull*.

Mansfield, Lynda Gianforte & Christopher H. Waldmann, MA, LPC, *Don't Touch My Heart*, Pinon Press, 1994.

Peterson, Janelle, RN, *The Invisible Road*, 1994.

Pickle, Paula, *Life In The Trenches: Survival Tactics*.

Randolph, Elizabeth, RN, Ph.D., *Children Who Shock And Surprise: A Guide To Attachment Disorders*, RFR Publications, 1994.

Streissguth, Ann P., Ph.D., *Understanding The Occurrence Of Secondary Disabilities In Clients With Fetal Alcohol Syndrome (FAS) And Fetal Alcohol Effects (FAE) Final Report*, University of Washington School of Medicine, Fetal Alcohol and Drug Unit.

The Attachment Center at Evergreen, Inc. & Carole A. McKelvey, *Give Them Roots, Then Let Them Fly*, Morris Publishing, 1995.

Verrier, Nancy Newton, *The Primal Wound — Understanding The Adopted Child*, Gateway Press, Inc., 1994.

Wadsworth, Barry J., *Piaget's Theory Of Cognitive Development*, David McKay, New York, 1971.

Welch, Martha G. M.D., *Holding Time*.

Watkins, Connell and Associates. Current information. Evergreen, CO 80439.